our
Environment

Energy

Bonnie Juettner

KIDHAVEN PRESS
A part of Gale, Cengage Learning

GALE
CENGAGE Learning™

Detroit • New York • San Francisco • New Haven, Conn • Waterville, Maine • London

© 2005 Gale, a part of Cengage Learning

For more information, contact
KidHaven Press
27500 Drake Rd.
Farmington Hills, MI 48331-3535
Or you can visit our Internet site at gale.cengage.com

LIBRARY OF CONGRESS CATALOGING-IN-PUBLICATION DATA

Juettner, Bonnie
  Energy / by Bonnie Juettner
    v. cm.—(Our environment)
  Includes bibliographical references and index.
  Contents: What does the world use for energy?—How is energy managed?—
  Are we running out of energy?—What will happen in the future?
    ISBN 0-7377-1821-8 (hardback : alk. paper)
  1. Power resources—Juvenile literature. 2. Energy industries—Juvenile literature.
  [1. Power resources. 2. Energy industries.] I. Title. II. Series.
    HD9502.A2J84 2004
    333.79—dc21

                                                                          2003000876

Printed in the United States of America
  4 5 6 7 12 11 10 09 08

contents

Chapter One

What Does the World Use for Energy?

Energy is the ability to do work. You do work when you run to catch the school bus. The bus does work when it carries you to school. The school furnace does work when it heats your classroom. Each time work gets done, energy is being used.

Your body gets energy from food. But your school bus, and probably your school heating system, get their energy from **fossil fuels**. Fossil fuels are the energy source that people in the United States, and the world, depend on most. The electricity for your school, however, might come from another source. It could come from a fossil fuel–burning electric plant, but it could also come from a nuclear power plant, a dam that makes electricity from the power of moving water, or even a wind farm.

Fossil Fuels

Many people think that fossil fuels, such as coal, oil, and natural gas, are the remains of dead dinosaurs. Actually, fossil fuels are even older. They are the remains of plants and animals that lived more than 300 million years ago, when the only animals on the earth were sea life, amphibians, and the earliest reptiles.

The windmills on a large wind farm like this one can create enough electricity to power thousands of homes.

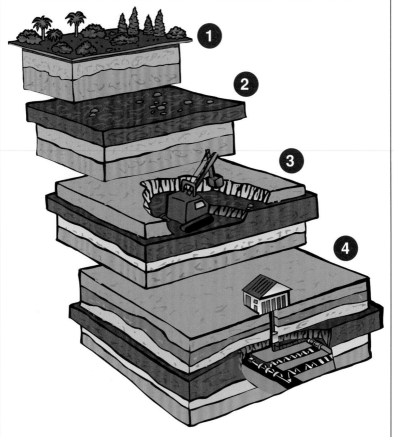

From Plants to Energy Source: How Coal Is Formed

1 Forming coal takes millions of years. As plants and trees die, they fall into water and are covered with layers of mud.

2 Layers of sediment, which contain minerals, bury the plants and dry them out, forming peat. Peat can be burned and used as fuel.

3 More layers of sediment are added. Heat and pressure turn the peat into soft coal. This soft coal can be dug from shallow pits in the earth.

4 As more layers are added, more heat and pressure make the coal harder, but push it deeper into the earth. Mines must be dug deep into the earth to remove the coal.

Fossil fuels formed slowly. First, the sun's light and heat traveled to the earth. Energy in the form of light and heat is called **electromagnetic radiation**. Ancient plants converted the sun's radiation into chemical energy through photosynthesis.

When ancient plants and animals died, some of them sank to the bottom of seas and were buried under layers of sediment. As the plant and animal matter decayed, high temperatures, combined with the pressure of the weight of sediments and water above them, forced oxygen out. Some of the decayed matter turned into **peat**, rotting plant matter that has been pressed into a dark colored mass of fibers, and then coal. And some turned into hydrocarbon, in the form of liquid oil or natural gas. These were then stored within the earth for millions of years. These fossil fuels are very useful to people today.

Combustion

Because the energy in fossil fuels is chemical energy, a chemical process must be used to release it. Combustion, or burning, is the process that is used. Combustion converts the chemical energy to heat. Then the energy can be used to heat a building or convert the heat to another form of energy, such as mechanical energy or electrical energy. Mechanical energy is energy that will make the moving parts of a machine move. Electrical energy is energy that takes the form of electricity.

Burning fossil fuels is such an easy and efficient way to get energy that fossil fuels are the energy source we use the most. The world gets 87 percent of its energy from fossil fuels.

Nuclear Energy

Nuclear energy is energy that is stored in the bonds that hold the nucleus of an atom together. During World War II, scientists figured out how to split apart the nucleus of an atom and release the energy that is stored there. This process is called **fission**. At first, people used this knowledge to make nuclear bombs, weapons of mass destruction.

This turbine at a nuclear power plant converts the energy of steam into electricity.

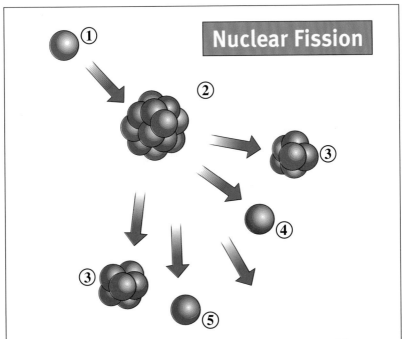

Nuclear Fission

Fission is the splitting of a heavy atom into two smaller parts. The energy created from the fission of an atom can be used to power nuclear reactors. The fission process begins when a tiny particle (1) is sent smashing into a heavy atom (2), breaking it apart into two smaller atoms (3). When the larger atom is split, it not only creates smaller atoms but also releases some extra electrons (4) and neutrons (5). These spare electrons and neutrons are used for energy.

Later, scientists developed other ways to use the energy. By slowing down the **nuclear reaction**, workers in a nuclear power plant can control it. They use some of the energy to boil water and make steam, and they contain the rest of the energy in rods filled with water or graphite.

A power plant can use either fossil fuels or nuclear power. In a power plant that burns fossil fuels, the burning fuels give off heat that is used to boil water. Steam coming off the water turns the blades of a **turbine**, converting the heat energy into mechanical energy. The turbine is connected to an electrical generator. As the turbine turns, it converts the mechanical energy into electrical energy. A nuclear power plant works the same way, except that the water is boiled by heat given off from uranium or plutonium atoms when they are split. The world gets 17 percent of its electricity this way, and some countries, like France and Lithuania, get more than 70 percent of their electricity this way.

Waterwheels and Dams

Wind and water energy are two of the oldest forms of energy used by humans. One of the earliest ways to harness this energy, begun two thousand years ago, was waterwheels. These wheels provided energy to grind grain in mills. Some historians think that waterwheels were the first machines. In the 1200s, people copied the waterwheel design to make windmills.

In ancient times, people placed a waterwheel in a river, knowing that the wheel would turn as long as the river's current remained strong. Today, waterwheels are part of a system that includes a dam and reservoir. The dam holds back the river's water, creating a large lake, or reservoir. Engineers can open gates in the dam to regulate water flow.

When the water pours through the gates of the dam, it hits blades that are connected to a turbine —the modern-day waterwheel. The turbine spins

The hydroelectric power plant inside Nevada's Hoover Dam contains seventeen turbines and provides electricity to three states.

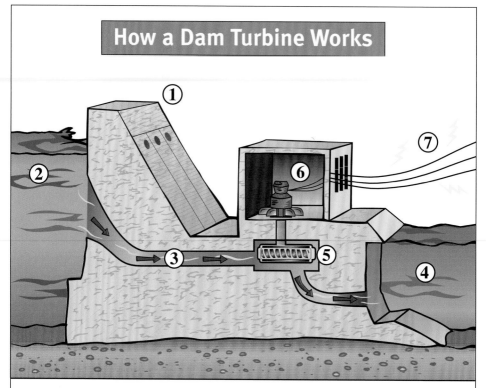

How a Dam Turbine Works

A dam (1) is built to hold back the water in a river to form a lake (2). The water from the lake passes through pipes (3) in the dam and exits down the river from the dam (4). The movement through the pipes turns a turbine blade (5). The turbine is attached to an electrical generator (6) that creates electricity when turned, and the electricity is sent out over power lines (7) to homes and businesses.

and converts the mechanical energy of the falling water into electrical energy, which can flow to a power plant. A power plant that gets its energy this way is called a **hydroelectric** power plant. Power from hydroelectric plants supplies 19 percent of the world's electricity.

The wheel design can also be used to harness the energy of wind. Wind energy is commonly used in the United States to pump water from wells in rural areas. But it can also be used to generate electricity. Wind energy is less reliable as a source of electricity because the wind does not blow all the time, and when it does blow, it does not always blow at high enough speeds to produce electricity. But wind energy can be used to add to, or supplement, energy from other sources.

In some parts of the United States and Europe, electricity is produced at large wind farms. Wind farms have many windmills. Thousands of windmills cover miles of land on these farms. Even in the United States, however, wind energy provides only about 4 percent of our energy. Wind energy is not a large contributor to the world's energy today. However, in years to come that may change. Wind farms are expanding quickly—wind energy is the fastest growing energy source in the world.

The amount of energy used in the world is growing all the time. In 1997, the world used a total amount of energy that was the equivalent of over 5.8 billion tons of oil. In 2020, scientists expect the world to use the equivalent of over 9.1 billion tons of oil. Every time that people think of a new way to use energy, they must also figure out what source of energy they will use.

chapter two

How Is Energy Managed?

People all over the world use energy. The form of energy that is used the most around the world, fossil fuel, is often mined by people in one country and sold to people in another country. As a result, energy use is managed by the free market system. This means that the amount of energy used by people and countries is not set by laws or governments. Instead, it varies depending on the demand for energy—the amount of energy that people want to use—and the supply of energy— the amount of energy that is available to buy. People and industries tend to use the energy source that best fits their needs and that they can obtain the most cheaply.

Who Uses Energy and What Do They Use?

Most fossil fuel is used by the industrialized countries of the world. In 2001, for example, the top four oil-consuming countries were the United States, Japan, China, and Germany. The United States used 19.7 million barrels of oil per day, Japan used 5.4 million, China 4.9 million, and Germany 2.8 million. These are countries where many people live in

A worker inspects a small section of an eight-hundred-mile-long oil pipeline in Alaska.

cities and work in factories. In industrialized countries, people rely on fossil fuels to produce heat and electricity. More than half of the homes in the United States, for example, are heated by natural gas. Many of these homes also use natural gas as fuel for cooking, providing hot water, and drying clothes.

Although much energy in industrialized countries is used to provide heat and electricity, far more fossil fuel is used by industry. Factories use fossil fuels as a raw material to make many products. Natural gas is an ingredient in paint, plastic, and even in film for cameras. Petroleum (crude oil that has been processed) is an ingredient in ink, crayons, bubble gum, dishwashing liquid, and tires. Petroleum also is important to the transportation industry as an ingredient in gasoline and jet fuel. Coal is one of the most important fuels used by industry, because it can be baked in hot furnaces to make coke, a substance used in making iron and steel. Industrialized countries depend on steel because it is used to build bridges, buildings, automobiles, machine parts, and of course many tools that we use every day, such as cooking pots.

Fuel for Factories

Factories also use fossil fuels in furnaces. Fossil fuels can be burned to produce very hot temperatures, hot enough to melt various kinds of metal. Then the liquid metal can be poured into molds and cooled to produce metal tools and parts. Fossil

Plastics are made from fossil fuels. These colored plastic pellets will be melted and formed into toys and other products.

fuels are also burned to heat water and produce steam, which can be used to turn a turbine and produce electricity.

In developing countries, countries that do not have as much industry and technology as industrialized countries, energy use is different. In developing countries such as India, South Africa, and Mexico, most people live in rural areas. In fact, more than half the world's population lives in rural areas, with more than 90 percent of the world's rural population living in developing countries. In these areas, most people (95 percent in some countries) depend on **biomass**—wood, other kinds of plant matter, and animal manure—for energy. They burn biomass in open fireplaces for cooking and heating.

Air Pollution

Both the fossil fuels used by industries and the biomass used in rural areas pollute the air. However, different fuels pollute differently. In cities, half of all air pollution comes from motor vehicles, because burning gasoline produces carbon monoxide, a gas that can cause headaches, nausea, and even death if people breathe too much of it. Natural gas is burned in large quantities in cities too, but natural gas burns much more cleanly than gasoline.

In rural areas, most air pollution is not outside, but inside. Burning biomass materials inside a home, for cooking, lighting, or heating, increases the number of small, fine particles in the air. When people breathe the air in these homes, they are more likely to develop lung infections or asthma. Women exposed to high levels of wood smoke are just as

Burning charcoal to barbecue food can pollute the air and cause health problems.

likely to develop lung cancer as if they smoked cigarettes. Pregnant women exposed to smoke are more likely to miscarry or have babies with low birth weights. And children who spend too much time in a smoky environment are more likely to develop diseases and to die of them.

In recent years, both industrialized countries and developing countries have begun to generate additional energy in a way that does not pollute the air. They have started building hydroelectric power plants. However, although hydroelectric plants can provide electricity, they cannot provide power for motor vehicles or heat furnaces to the temperatures

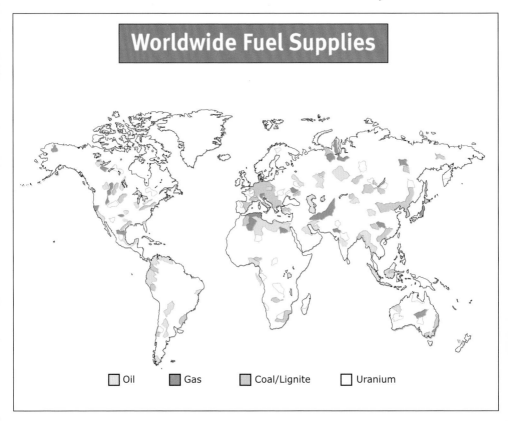

Worldwide Fuel Supplies

☐ Oil   ■ Gas   ☐ Coal/Lignite   ☐ Uranium

necessary for smelting iron. Currently, people must rely on fossil fuels for these purposes. And clean electricity does not help the 2 billion people who do not have access to electricity. Two-thirds of people living in rural areas do not have electricity, so they have no choice but to rely on biomass to provide light as well as heat and cooking energy.

Who Supplies Energy?

Fossil fuels are not deposited evenly throughout the world. There are reserves of fossil fuel in many places around the world, however. The largest deposits of crude oil, the fossil fuel people depend on most, are in the Middle East. No other area comes close to having as much oil as the Middle East does, with its 659 billion barrels of oil in proven reserves. The reserves in the rest of the world, all put together, total only 348 billion barrels. Of those, the United States has 22 billion barrels. Several areas have more oil than the United States: South America (79 billion barrels), Africa (73 billion), Central Asia (59 billion), Mexico (50 billion), and the Pacific Rim countries of Southeast Asia (44 billion).

Why Do Energy Costs Keep Changing?

Energy costs can change for two reasons. When the supply of fossil fuels increases, as it does when new reserves of fuel are discovered, the price goes

Sometimes demand for fuel is higher than the supply, which causes gas shortages like this one in 1974.

down. When the supply decreases, either because some reserves are running dry or because oil producers decide not to put as much oil on the market, the price goes up. When the demand for oil goes up—because of increasing world population or because more countries are industrializing—the price also goes up. This is called the law of supply and demand. When the demand is high and the supply is low, prices are high. When the supply is high and the demand is low, prices are low.

chapter three

Are We Running Out of Energy?

Many people worry about what would happen if the world ran out of energy. Of course, technically, the world cannot run out of energy. That would violate the laws of physics, which state that energy can never be created or destroyed—it can only change from one form into another. However, some forms of energy are easier for people to use than others. The world currently depends on fossil fuels for 87 percent of its energy needs. It is impossible for people to use up all the energy in the world, but it is possible to use up most fossil-fuel sources. There are forms of energy, however, that cannot be used up. These forms are called **renewable** sources of energy.

Renewable and Nonrenewable Forms of Energy

Renewable forms of energy are energy sources that can be replaced as they are used up. In the late 1800s, people in the United States got 90 percent of their energy from a renewable source: wood. Wood is renewable because it is possible to grow new trees. Solar power is also classified as a renewable energy source. It will continue to be supplied to the earth as long as the sun keeps producing energy. Scientists estimate that humans can rely on the sun for another 5 billion years—long enough that no one needs to

Rows of solar panels collecting the sun's energy provide electricity to a public park in Utah.

worry about running out of solar energy. Wind and water power are renewable as well—people can use them as long as the wind continues to blow and the water cycle continues to operate.

Fossil fuels are not renewable even though, technically, more fossil fuels are being formed all the time. Unfortunately, the process of fossil-fuel formation takes 100 million years. Because it takes so long to make fossil fuels, they are considered a **nonrenewable** form of energy. Nonrenewable energy is energy that people cannot make more of. Like energy that comes from fossil fuels, nuclear energy is also considered nonrenewable. That is because nuclear plants use a rare form of uranium as fuel.

How Long Will Fossil Fuels Last?

Since the world relies heavily on fossil fuels, which cannot last forever, someday it will become necessary to make different choices about energy. Nobody knows how long the fossil-fuel supply will last, because nobody knows what undiscovered reserves of fossil fuel the world may still have or how much the demand for fossil fuel will increase. The U.S. government estimates that Americans (who already use 25 percent of the world's energy) will use 33 percent more oil and 45 percent more natural gas in the next twenty years. Overall, world energy demand is expected to increase 1.7 percent per year from 2000 to 2030. If so, the increase alone will equal two-thirds of the current demand. Oil demand will increase even more—by 2.2 percent every year.

Just in case there is a shortage, the United States saves oil in a large reservoir, the Strategic Petroleum Reserve. The reserve, which can hold up to 700 million barrels of oil, is the largest emergency oil stockpile in the world. Many scientists expect shortages of petroleum will begin to occur by the middle of the twenty-first century. The International Energy Agency, for example, has stated that new oil reserves will have to be discovered to meet the increase in world oil demand in the years from now until 2030. Natural gas should last a little longer.

U.S. Strategic Petroleum Reserve

ARKANSAS

TENN.

OKLAHOMA

MISSISSIPP

The U.S. government has millions of barrels of oil stored in the Strategic Petroleum Reserve.

LOUISIANA

West Hackberry

Bayou Choctaw

TEXAS

Big Hill

Bryan Mound

Gulf of Mexico

People continue to depend on fossil fuels like gasoline because they are cheap and readily available.

Coal, however, will last more than two hundred years, until the twenty-third century. Coal can be burned to supply heat and electricity, and it can be used by factories. However, because coal is solid, it is harder to mine, and it cannot be used as fuel for cars, trucks, airplanes, or ships.

How Does a Free Market Affect Our Choices About Energy?

Could people just give up using nonrenewable forms of energy and switch to renewable ones? After all, renewable forms of energy will not run out, and they often are less harmful to the environment than nonrenewable forms. Why do families and industries continue using fossil fuels?

Right now, the biggest reason fossil fuels continue to be used is that they are still readily available and cheap. People still can heat their homes and power their cars more cheaply by using fossil fuels, and industries can still power factories more cheaply by using fossil fuels. In the long run, renewable forms of energy cost less than using fossil fuels. But the process of converting to renewable energy sources can be expensive.

For example, to use solar energy, you need a device for collecting and storing energy from sunlight. You also need devices for converting the solar energy to electricity, if you plan to use it for electricity. The North Carolina Solar Center (NCSC) has set up a model solar house, which is fairly small and gets half its electricity from solar energy. The cost of installing a system like the one in the NCSC's model house is $32,000. The average monthly electricity bill in North Carolina is $87, so a house that saves half that, or $43.50, per month, would take 753 months, or almost 63 years, to earn back that $32,000. On the other hand, solar houses are not much more expensive to build than traditional houses. It only costs 2.5 percent more to build a solar house in North Carolina than it does to build a traditional house. In some parts of the country, solar houses cost even less to build.

Finding New Fuel Sources

If you wanted to convert a car to run on electricity instead of gasoline, it would cost you between ten thousand and twenty thousand dollars. Or you could buy an electric car for thirty-four thousand to forty-four thousand dollars. If you wanted to charge your electric car using power derived from solar or wind sources, you would also need to invest several thousand dollars in a solar or wind turbine generator. A few families can afford to spend this much money converting their homes and vehicles, but most will wait until the price of fossil fuels is too high to bear.

In the meantime, scientists and engineers are researching new ways to extract more fossil fuel from existing reserves. One option is to use shale oil, a solid form of oil that is more difficult to use than liquid petroleum. The western part of the United

States has a deposit of shale that contains between 600 billion and 2 trillion barrels of oil. Unfortunately, shale oil is expensive to mine, and it contains much less energy than other fossil fuels—about eight times less than coal. As long as oil prices remain low, oil companies do not want to spend the money to extract shale oil, but if oil prices rise, they are likely to begin mining shale oil.

Another option is tar sands, sand soaked with bitumen, with is a very thick kind of crude oil. Recently, engineers have found cost-effective ways to

Shale rock (left) contains large amounts of organic material that can be converted into oil (right).

extract oil from tar sands. However, to produce one barrel of oil, miners must process two tons of tar sand.

It is easy to see why many people and companies prefer to use fossil fuel as long as they can. However, as fossil fuels get used up, their price will rise. Also, scientists are continually developing new technology that makes use of renewable energy sources in ways that are more efficient. As fossil-fuel prices rise, renewable energy prices are beginning to drop. If this trend continues long enough, eventually fossil fuels will be more expensive than renewable energy sources. When that happens, people may start to use energy from sources that they can hardly imagine using today.

Chapter Four

What Will Happen in the Future?

What will people use for energy when it becomes too expensive to use fossil fuels? Probably, people will use energy from a variety of sources. They will almost certainly turn to solar power, wind farms, and hydroelectric power. The technology for these things exists and is already in use today. But can you imagine an energy generator that sits on your kitchen counter, taking up no more space than a toaster? Or a generator that burns garbage from your kitchen or sewage from your toilet? Or a generator that harnesses the internal warmth of the earth itself? These options may sound like science fiction, but someday they may become science fact.

Nuclear Fusion

Nuclear **fusion** is the opposite of nuclear fission, the reaction that is used in nuclear power plants. In nuclear fusion, instead of splitting an atom, scientists cause two atoms to collide. When the two atoms crash into each other, energy is given off. Unlike nuclear fission, which uses a rare form of uranium, nuclear fusion can use deuterium, an element that can be found in seawater. To generate high amounts of energy, fusion must occur at very high temperatures, such as the temperatures in the sun. (Stars generate energy through nuclear fusion.)

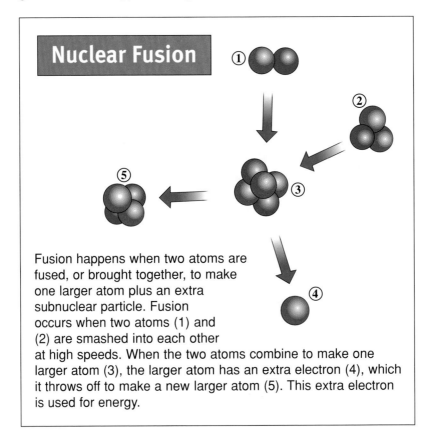

Nuclear Fusion

Fusion happens when two atoms are fused, or brought together, to make one larger atom plus an extra subnuclear particle. Fusion occurs when two atoms (1) and (2) are smashed into each other at high speeds. When the two atoms combine to make one larger atom (3), the larger atom has an extra electron (4), which it throws off to make a new larger atom (5). This extra electron is used for energy.

Since 1999, scientists have been able to make nuclear fusion happen using tabletop devices. They did it by flashing laser pulses, each a trillionth of a second long, at clusters of deuterium. In 2002, a team of researchers succeeded in producing nuclear fusion in a tabletop machine that was the size of three stacked coffee cups. This device used bubbles, which scientists bombarded with sound waves, producing flashes of light temperatures as hot as the surface of the sun. If scientists can find a way to harness the energy of nuclear fusion, it could become an almost endless, environmentally clean form of energy. That is a big "if." Currently, nuclear fusion takes more energy to produce than the amount of energy it gives off. Years of research may lie ahead before tabletop nuclear fusion becomes routine, if it ever does.

Waste to Energy

Converting waste to energy, however, is something people already have the technology to do. Waste falls into the category of renewable energy called biomass. It can include almost anything that people throw away and that can be burned to produce heat. Most of the solid waste that people throw in the garbage consists of paper, food, plant waste, and wood. These are all substances that can be burned, and they are a resource that cities have in large supply. People in the United States generate more than 200 million tons of garbage every year. Now, some landfills burn garbage to produce electricity. Like coal-burning power plants, these generators use heat from burning fuel to warm water and create steam. The steam can then be used to turn the blades of a turbine and generate electricity.

Some forms of biomass can be converted into a fluid fuel for burning, such as ethanol or methane.

A scientist experiments with a machine that converts waste paper into ethanol, a fluid fuel.

Ethanol is a type of alcohol made from corn. It can be used as a supplement to gasoline in cars. Ethanol has been used to supply power for cars for a long time. In fact, the 1908 Ford Model T could run on ethanol, gasoline, or a mixture of the two. Today, some parts of the United States require that motorists use a blend of ethanol and gasoline in their cars during the winter. This blend—10 percent ethanol and 90 percent gasoline—is called gasohol. As long as gasoline prices remain low enough, it will not be practical for drivers to switch to pure ethanol, because ethanol costs more and gets fewer miles per gallon than gasoline. One reason ethanol costs so much is that manufacturers must burn fossil fuels to produce it.

Methane

Biomass can also be converted to methane, a gas that is produced when bacteria cause wastes to rot. Methane can be harvested from algae, waste from farms and factories, sludge from sewage treatment plants, and decaying crops. Sewage can include liquid and solid waste from toilets, sinks, storm-water runoff, and so forth. There is a power generator at the city sewage plant in Boulder, Colorado, that burns methane from sewage and uses the heat to produce electricity. The sewage plant then sells the electricity to the city, earning about ninety-three thousand dollars a year from it.

Burning waste has several advantages—it uses up waste that would otherwise fill landfills, and it uses technology that already exists. But it does have a disadvantage: Burning fuel of any sort pollutes the air with particles of waste.

Energy from the Earth and the Moon

Some scientists hope to supplement humans' energy needs with energy from within the earth itself or from the moon. Energy from within the earth is called geothermal energy. And energy from the moon's gravity affects the earth in the form of ocean tides.

Geothermal energy occurs in two forms: steam that flows to the surface of the earth at hot springs or geysers, and hot rocks, granite that is warmed by heat flowing from the interior of the earth to the surface. Hot rocks can be as hot as four hundred degrees Fahrenheit. People have harnessed the energy of hot springs and geysers since the early 1900s. There are 204 power plants in the United States that use geothermal energy from steam, and the capital of Iceland, Reykjavik, is mostly heated by geothermal energy. Geothermal energy is safe and does not pollute the environment. But hot springs only occur in a few places on the earth's surface. Hot rocks, on the other hand, exist almost everywhere, but they are deep below the earth's crust. Scientists are working with drilling technology from the oil industry to find ways to pump water deep into these rocks. They

These fuel pellets are created from compressed garbage. The pellets are burned to create energy for electricity.

hope to use steam from the heated water to move the blades of electric turbines. So far, though, they have not found a way to do this that will not cost more than the electric energy would be worth.

Like energy from hot springs, tidal energy works best in particular locations. The moon's gravity pulls at the waters of the ocean everywhere, but some inlets, like Alaska's Cook Inlet, have particularly long tides. Tidal power plants operate like hydroelectric plants. The moving water turns the blades of a turbine to generate electricity. Currently, there are three tidal power plants in operation worldwide.

Turning Ideas into Action

Scientists have many ideas about how to provide energy to people in the future. People will eventually have to rely less on fossil fuels, but it is hard to predict what energy source will prove to be the most practical and cheapest replacement for those fuels. Think about your own community and how

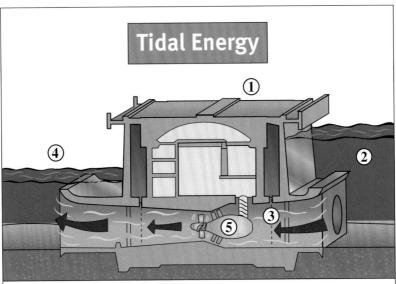

Tidal Energy

In areas where ocean tides rise and fall dramatically, the back-and-forth movement of the tides can be captured and used to power special turbines. In this diagram, a wall (1) has been built over the tide path. The high tide (2) passes through a tunnel (3) until it reaches the same level as the low tide (4). As the water passes through the tunnel, it turns a special turbine generator (5) which generates electricity for use in homes and businesses.

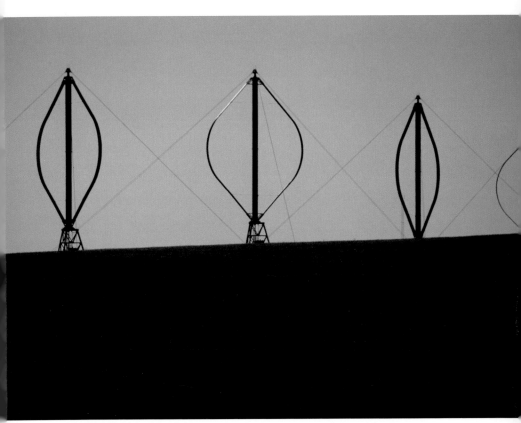

In windy parts of the world, high-tech windmills like these can provide a cheap source of energy.

it might change. Do you live near a coastal inlet or in a very windy part of the country? What do you think would be the most practical source of energy for your community? Your imagination is the limit!

Glossary

biomass: Matter that once was alive and can be burned to produce energy.

electromagnetic radiation: Energy that travels through space in waves, often taking the form of heat or light.

energy: The ability to do work.

fission: Splitting apart an atom.

fossil fuel: Fuels such as oil, coal, and natural gas, which are the remains of plants and animals that lived more than 300 million years ago.

fusion: Connecting more than one atom to make a new substance and give off energy.

hydroelectric: Power that is generated from the energy of running water.

nonrenewable: An energy source that can be used up.

nuclear reaction: A reaction between the center of an atom and a particle that it is bombarded with, creating a new substance.

peat: Decomposed vegetable matter in the very early stages of turning into coal. When burned as biomass, peat produces one-third to one-half as much heat as coal.

renewable: An energy source that cannot be used up.

turbine: A machine that converts the energy of moving water to electricity.

For Further Exploration

Books

Neil Ardley, *Science Book of Energy*. Toronto: Doubleday Canada, 1992.

Jack Challonger, *Dorling Kindersley Eyewitness Books: Energy*. New York: Dorling Kindersley, 2000.

Allan Fowler, *Energy from the Sun*. Chicago: Childrens Press, 1998.

Linda Jacobs, *Letting Off Steam: The Story of Geothermal Energy*. Minneapolis: Carolrhoda Books, 1989.

Barbara Shaw McKinney, *Pass the Energy, Please*. Nevada City, CA: Dawn, 2000.

Web Sites

California Energy Commission (www.energyquest. ca.gov). The Web site of the California Energy Commission includes games, a library of links, and weekly energy news.

Danish Wind Industry Association (www. windpower.org). A Web site explaining how wind energy works.

Office of Energy Efficiency and Renewable Energy (www.eren.doe.gov). This site gives details about how each aspect of a solar home works.

U.S. Department of Energy (www.eia.doe.gov). This Web site includes detailed information about renewable and nonrenewable sources of energy. It also has links to Web sites that include more detailed information.

Index

Picture credits

Cover Image: © Lester Lefkowitz/CORBIS
AP/Wide World Photos, 25
© Alex Bartel/Photo Researchers, Inc., 8
© Martin Bond/Photo Researchers, Inc., 39
Lee Foster/Lonely Planet Images, 15
© Owen Franken/CORBIS, 22
© Dave G. Houser/CORBIS, 19
© Bob Krist/CORBIS, 17
© Lester Lefkowitz/CORBIS, 11
PhotoDisc, 5, 41
Suzanne Santillan, 6, 9, 12, 20, 27, 34, 40
© Tom Stewart/CORBIS, 28
© U.S. Department of Energy/Photo Researchers,
   Inc., 31, 36

About the
Author

Bonnie Juetner is a writer and editor of children's reference books and educational videos. Originally from McGrath, Alaska, she currently lives in Kenosha, Wisconsin. This is her third book.